AF430751

@ANISSA_SAFIA_BOOKS

Dear Readers,

This book is an open letter from a mom who works long hours at the office, to her child she sends to daycare.

This book is dedicated to the hard working moms out there and the sweet children who miss their mommies and don't understand why mommy is not around as much as they would like.

We all do our best to our own capacity.
Mom guilt is REAL!

We hope our book creates a little joy and serves as a comfort for you and your loved ones.

Remember moms, don't be too hard on yourself.
We do what we can.
Your kids love you!

Love,
A mom & a loving auntie.

Before Sunrise

Everyday Mama wakes up before the sunrise,
just to watch my baby sleep.

Look how beautiful you are.

Today is my workday and your school day.
When you wake up and your eyes open wide,
Mama quickly gives you a big hug and kiss.

"Good morning my Sunshine!"
Mama says, "you must be
starving!"

Ready, Set, Go!

We have a big healthy breakfast together.
Still a little tired, even our food looks a
little sleepy.

We take a nice warm bath together
because somebody's armpits are smelly...

We do not want to walk around with an
itchy body, be seen scratching ourselves and
scaring away our friends!

Then we brush our teeth together because somebody's mouth is also smelly...

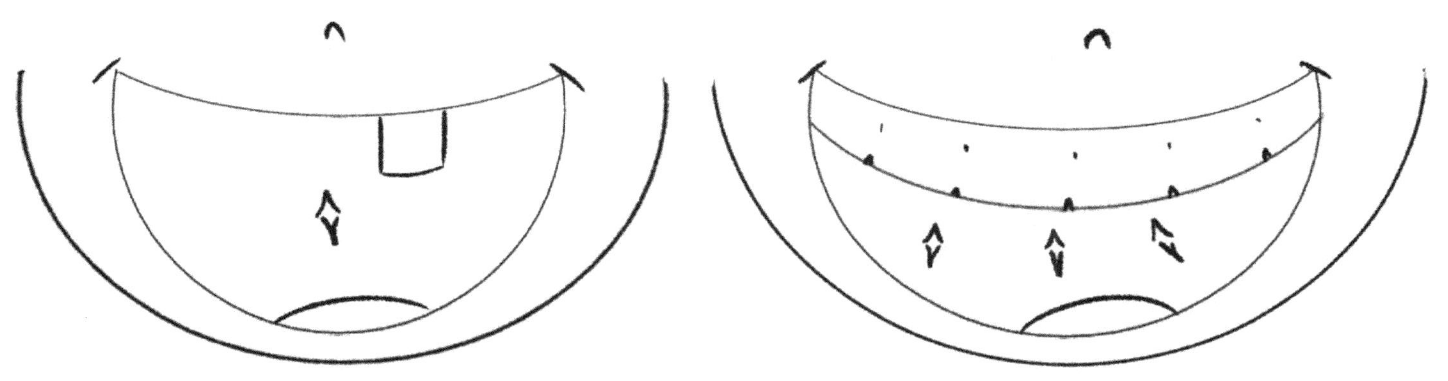

We do not want to scare away our friends because of smelly mouths!!

Then lastly, we get dressed together.
"How would you like to do your hair this
morning?" Mama asks you.

You carry your school bag.
I carry my handbag.

After we are all dressed up, Mama tells
you to talk to yourself in the mirror.

Repeat after me:
"I am smart. I am kind.
I am important.
Today will be a good day!"

Time To Leave The House!

If I could, I would love to hold you in my arms on the drive to your school. But safety first! Children must sit in the car seat.

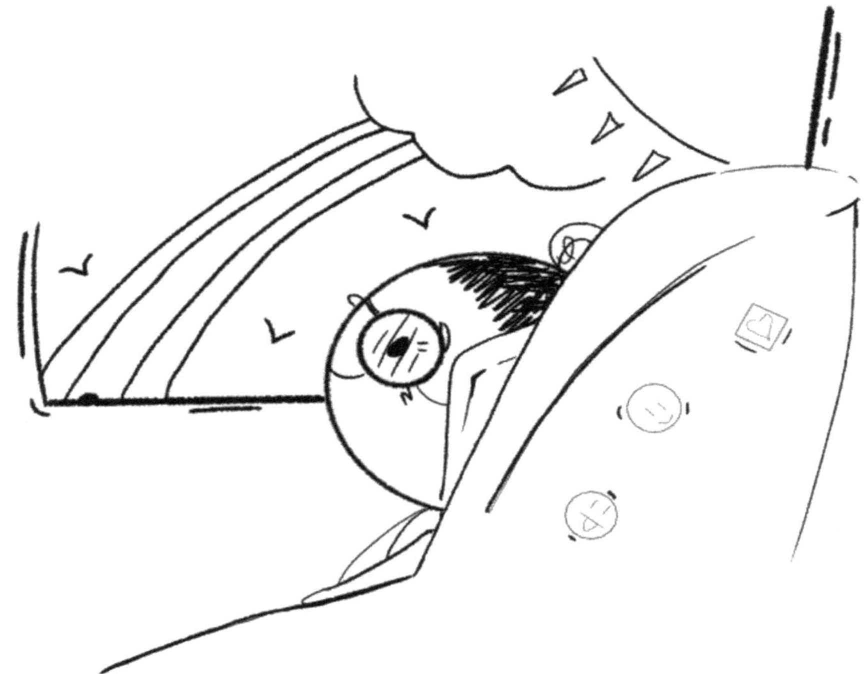

Don't worry, Mama made your car seat super comfortable and cool just for you!
"What music would you like to listen to this morning, sweetheart?" Mama asks you.

At Your School

Before Mama walks you to school,
I always give you a big, fat hug and a big, fat kiss!

I tell you "I love you with all my heart and I will
miss you all day, my little pumpkin."

Then you turn around and look at all your friends waiting for you at school. Mama feels so happy every time you run off shouting. "th'ee yew latooor alligatooooor! SNAP SNAP".

You completely forgot about Mama! I am glad. Go have fun!

At My Office

On the way to my office from your school, I already start missing you so much.

As soon as I reach the office, I always check the time. I hope time goes by quickly today so I can be with you again.

I meet other Moms who also work. I talk about you. They talk about their own children. I always share about how kind, caring and FAST you are.

During my lunch break at the office, I wonder if you have eaten too.

I wonder if you had finished all the food I had packed for you and if your tummy is full, big and round.

During my free time at the
office, I plan when to take
my family for a holiday.

Should we go on our holiday during Spring, when the flowers bloom?

Summer, when it's warm and the sun is out?

Autumn,
when the leaves
start falling?

Winter,
when we can
dance on ice?

Still At The Office (Half Day)

Mama can't keep you out of my mind! I always worry about you, my darling.

I wonder if you are playing happily with your friends.
Are you sharing your toys?
Are your friends being nice to you?
Tell me every single thing that happens in your day at school.

I wonder if you hurt
yourself and need me
to kiss your boo boo's.

Are you okay?
Tell me if you're
in pain..

I wonder if you
need a hug, a kiss
or an applause.

Do You Know Why Mama Wants to Work?

I want to buy you yummy food to make you grow tall, big, strong, and healthy.

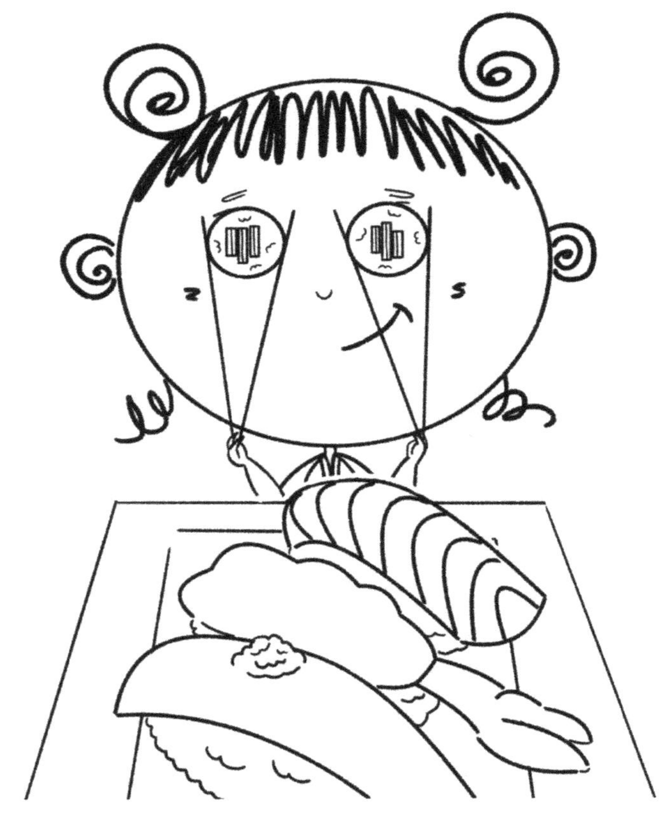

Please don't waste good food.
Finish what you can and keep the rest for tomorrow.

To buy you new
clothes, to keep you
warm and feel
beautiful.

The most
beautiful thing
you can wear is a
big smile and a
kind heart.

When you are sick,
I want to send you to see the best doctors at
the best hospitals to take good care of you.

Of course,
there is nothing
like a mother's
love, which is
FREE!

I want to send you to good schools
to learn new things so your brain
can grow.

Of course, you need to also work hard
and do all your homework.
NO CHEATING!

I want to give you a
beautiful home to keep
you safe, warm and
comfortable.

But please don't forget
to flush the toilet once
you are done!

Mama wants to take you around the world to play with snow...

Watch out for the big snow ball!

...and build sandcastles on the beach.

Help! Sand is getting in my eyes and clothes! Water! Water!

NO TOUCHY!

I want to take you places
where you can ride
horses...

Wow, what big
nostrils!

elephants...

Gosh, what big
ears!

ships...

Look!
A mermaid?!

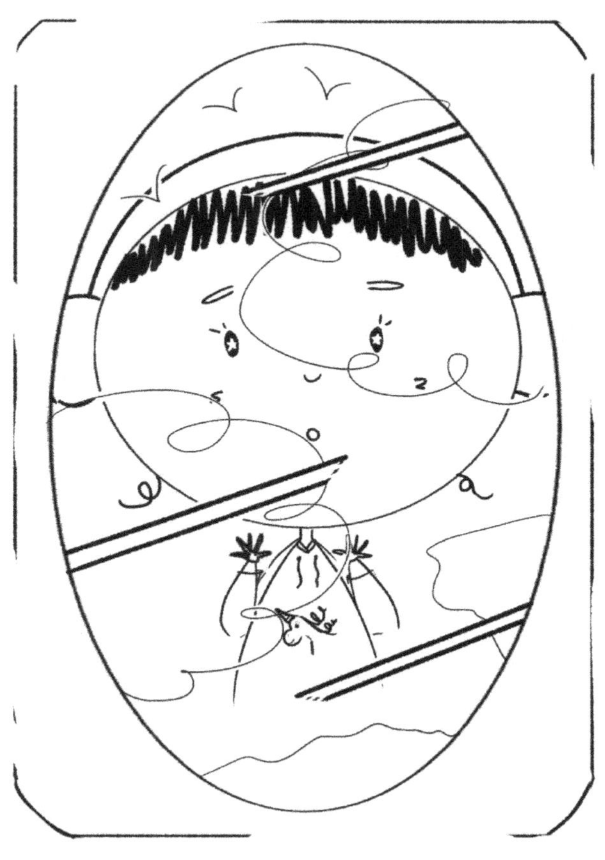

aeroplanes...

Whoa!
Cotton candy in
the sky?!

and parachutes!

Look baby, you can fly!
Are you a bird now?

28

Mama wants to bring you to play and have fun in big theme parks...

Even though rollercoasters make me sick...

Mama wants to watch movies with you at big cinemas and eat some yummy snacks!

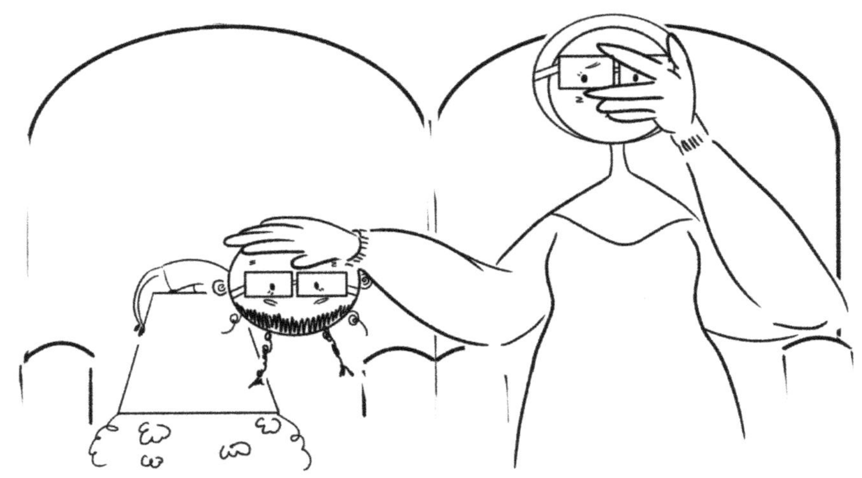

...why do you like to watch scary movies?

Buy you cool toys!

....even though they take up alot of space and end up scattered all over the house.

Time To Go Home

It's 5.30pm.
Mama rockets to school
to pick my baby up.

Oh no! On the way home, there is a traffic jam! Everyone is rushing to pick their children up from school.

Hang in there cupcake, Mama is on the way.
"Move, man! I want to see my baby!" Mama yells.

I finally arrive and see you playing catch with your friends. All of you were shouting and laughing. You must have had so much fun at school today!

When the door opens, Mama welcomes you in my arms with "Hello again my love!". Mama is the happiest when I see your face!

"How was your day, my darling?" I ask you this every day after school pick-up. "Learn anything new? Made any mistakes today?" Don't be afraid to make mistakes. We all learn from our mistakes! Mama too!

Home-Sweet-Home

Mama gives you a nice and warm shower.

I know you played in the mud today! Mama has 3 eyes and can see everything.

Then I change you into
fresh new clothes to
wear.

I cook you a yummy dinner. Mac n' Cheese? Rice with Curry Chicken?
"You have to eat vegetables and fruits too, okay? They're good for you, don't gag! NO VOMITING!"

Then we sit around the table and start eating together...

"Mmm...crunchy... Good! Booo... Sweet... Bad!"

...playing together...

"I always lose to you!
Let me win for once,
please."

YAWN
...and doing our homework together.
"Stop falling asleep! Now I am going to fall asleep..."
"...noooooo...."
"Zzzzzzzzzzzzz"

39

Sleeping Time

We always need to get a good nights rest.

When we rest, we let our body rest, our brain rest and get the energy we need to get through the next day.

But don't sleep too much or you will wake up as a vampire!

Before You Drift Into Dreamland

Mama wants to tell you:

I am so PROUD OF YOU, my sweet baby. I know today was not easy but you made it through the day. Your teacher told me you were being so kind to all your friends and you learnt so much in school.

You are IMPORTANT.
You are SMART.
You are KIND.
You are AWESOME.

Mama is always working hard
To keep you SAFE
To keep you HEALTHY
To keep you HAPPY

I love you so much.